How to

be Happy

by Francesca Hepton

ISBN: 978-1-9999126-4-2

For anyone who wants to:

Put a skip back in their step
See life through positive eyes

Also by Francesca Hepton
*in the **How to**... series:*

Save Money
Stop Smoking and Start Living
Give up Drinking and be part of the world again
Look Young and be more grateful, grounded + gorgeous
Get Fit with Reiki and Music

First published in 2017
by Babili Books
a division of Babili Services Ltd

CONTENTS

How to be Happy

Introduction

Feeling low? Feeling like it is all pointless? Feeling demoralised?

Wouldn't mind having some luck? Wouldn't mind things going your way for a change? Wouldn't mind laughing again?

The good news is, you have already done the hard part.

You've reached out. A lot of people who feel down or low do not want help – they want to be left alone. By seeking out a different voice or advice in the form of this book, you have already taken the hardest step.

Well done.

That step is a type of emotional self-recognition, i.e. recognising what kind of person you are. I take my hat off to you.

Now for the easy part. Your steps to happiness.

You still have a part to play here, but just follow the guide and help yourself to as much happiness as you can manage!

What is self-help?

By studying our "self" and the "ego states" that govern our decisions and emotions (Egolosophy©), we can better understand ourselves. With a better understanding of our "self" and our different "egos", we can then attain greater happiness by living a life that is true to our "self". When you are not living true to your "self", you are not in alignment, you are out of synch, nothing is harmonious and this brings about the internal imbalances and the unhappiness.

You become lost. That is why you need to reset your internal compass so you can make decisions that you believe in, rather than following decisions society or those around you make you feel you should be making.

In all my self-help guides, I ask my readers to take the reigns of their **own** life in their **own** hands. Whether it is conquering an addiction, how to get fit and eat healthily, how to look younger so you can feel better about yourself, how to save money so you can do things you want... they all work hand in hand. But **you are in charge. Don't wait for someone else to magically appear and solve your problems.**

Feel good about yourself and you will succeed, you will be happier, you will find that elusive inner peace. Just like there are many pieces to the puzzle of inner peace, there are likewise many facets to the concept of happiness. This guide does not pretend to encompass all of them.

It focuses primarily on **general happiness** and **enhancing optimism** rather than having you rolling around on the floor holding your sides, or on a more serious note, other aspects of the subject of happiness such as gratitude, compassion, supportive attachments, religious faith and so on. As you will appreciate, the subject is vast.

Let's focus on getting that skip back into your life. Go on, get happy!

CHAPTER 1   FOCUS

Your goal, the end game and how to get there.

We all need a bright future and a bright tomorrow to look forward to. Otherwise what are we living for? Perhaps more importantly we also need to be happy with where we are now (because today is yesterday's future... the one you were working towards, the present is the future you want).

If your present circumstances are not "b-**right**", then I want to help put that skip back into your step.

I want you to focus on that b-**right** future you want for yourself (and/or your loved ones), focus so hard it becomes a part of your everyday thoughts, so that it becomes a reality.

Resetting your internal compass is essential to being happy. You must be yourself. You must know what you want out of your life. But where do you start when you reset your internal compass? The key is **FOCUS**:

Find where you want to go.

Offload the superfluous.

Carry only what you need.

Understand yourself.

Stop worrying.

Keeping it simple is essential. Do not complicate your journey to happiness.

Be clear about what you want (later you will find help on ignoring all that noise from society, telling you what you want). Listen to yourself. Inside you is the key to your happiness. Not what the media or your parents and friends tell you. Only you know what makes you happy.

Whether it is getting that pink plastic jacket, a Mohican, a job at the bakers, going out with Timmy, setting up a stall at the Christmas market, having a tattoo, learning how to ski, getting your nose pierced, cross-dressing, writing music, starting your education again, becoming a groupie, living in a different country, buying some cheap platform boots – only you know what makes you tick, how you feel that buzz when you are shaking your thang on the dance floor, or have neatly flowering perennials in your front garden, a shiny Mustang on your drive, can do 100 jumps on your pogo stick – **ONLY YOU KNOW what gives you that buzz.**

Do not be told who to be!

Once you have filtered out the noise and chaos from the outside and have focused on what you want in order to be happy, or at least less sad, then you are ready to start your journey.

"All that we are is the result of what we have thought." **– Buddha**

I am not talking about any Jedi mind tricks. "Much easier than that it is my young Jedi." You simply have to carry a thought in your mind. No strenuous thinking or failed attempts at meditation. What I am referring to is having that focus of what you want in your mind as part of your everyday thoughts. Remind yourself of who you are or want to be and what you want out of your life.

When you know what you are aiming for it is all the easier to get there. You cannot take wrong turns because you are focused on your path. Your journey.

A better understanding of F-O-C-U-S with some examples:

Example 1

Sports

If you are a skier or a racing car driver or a tennis player (any sportsman really, including darts!), you know that where your eyes are focused is your ultimate destination. Sometimes it helps to look as far into the distance as possible to make that turn and take those bends with greater precision, speed and confidence.

Looking to the horizon on the racetrack, you will weave your way around the other competitors. You will not worry about the trivial bends that may slow you down, you will glide past them with your gaze firmly fixed on your furthest point of vision: Your goal.

If you distract yourself with too many things, you spread and dilute your energy. If you dedicate yourself to one project, one objective you will get so much more done.

By achieving your goal(s) you will find satisfaction, even happiness.

If you are not achieving your goal(s), you will become dissatisfied and disillusioned. This leads to listlessness and inertia. Keep focused.

Example 2:

The Six Harmonies:

Six Harmonies include harmonizing the body and heart/mind, heart/mind and intent, intent and Qi/energy, Qi/energy and spirit, spirit and movement, and movement and emptiness.

If you want to move forward, if you want change, it all starts with your intent. Your interior connects with your exterior. What is happening on the inside is reflected on the outside. Just like a smile shows you are happy, the actions you take, the decisions you make are reflections of what is going on in your mind. Your intent.

And back to the example, when you make a movement following the rules of the Six Harmonies, you are unifying your body and the strength comes not from your muscle but from your **focus and intent**.

As you turn on your axis (e.g. knees, hip joints, elbows, etc.) you enhance the power behind your every move/turn by looking at the furthest point in your direction of travel.

THE TRANSFER OF POWER FROM THE MENTAL TO THE PHYSICAL.

By focusing on your intent, looking at the furthest point of your vision and making the move once your body is in complete harmony, you will make the greatest impact and the strength for the move/change will be there. It is almost effortless.

You have to look inside to find your true strength, find what makes you tick and what makes you lose your self-control. Unleash your potential, don't be afraid to succeed. You are allowed to be happy. It is not a feeling reserved solely for an elite club where the grass is always greener, the sun always shines and the money rains from the sky.

If you take steps to understanding yourself, you can become master of your own destiny. We are not all destined to become stars or make our mark in history. Yet, we all deserve to experience happiness on this earth and if you feel that you are bereft, alone and down in the dumps, this guide will help steer you in the right direction to becoming a happier person through focus.

YOUR INTENT IS YOUR GOAL

First things first: DEFINE YOUR GOAL

To understand who you are and what you want out of life.

Not what others or society tells you. What **you** want and to go for it.

It can be as simple as being as good as your dance or Pilates teacher or better than your teacher or to be the next Victoria or David Beckham or to be the best cook in your family.

Whatever your benchmark is, if you get it, you fell like a winner and that is the essential secret to being happy.

Compromises are essential at times, but do not live a life of compromises, then neither you or the party/person you are compromising with will ever be satisfied because you'll never get what you actually wanted... just somewhere in the middle. Stick to what YOU want. Do not dilute your intent or your focus.

First step: Recognise when you are sad. Understand why. Or at least try to. This is essential. If you are in a "sad" or "low" mood, don't try to push yourself to be something you are not before you are ready. You could just make yourself feel worse through more disappointment and a spiralling feeling of inferiority and failure.

So stop! Take things slowly.

End goal: The end game is to enjoy every day of your life on this beautiful planet. Not to enjoy it the way you think you are supposed to or the way others tell you to enjoy it. To enjoy every day in YOUR own way. If you love working then having a busy work-filled day will make you happy, don't feel bad about that. Likewise, if you are having an off day, then recognise it, accept it and go with the flow, do not force yourself to shine that day. You'll shine all the brighter for it the next time.

Although it may sound obvious, you need to have an intent, a goal in mind so that you know what to aim for. All the times you feel low, ask yourself what it is that you are missing. It could be a partner, the unfulfilled ambition of starting your own company, wanting more time for yourself, stopping a bad habit, being fitter or feeling less "unfit", to be more proactive, to watch less TV, to get out of the relationship you are in, have a better rapport with your children, to learn a new skill, etc. Whatever it is that is making you feel low, you can lift yourself up through some positive action and changes to your routine towards achieving what you want.

It is easier than you think.

MAKE TODAY THE START OF YOUR END GOAL

CHAPTER 2   A STARTING POINT

Understanding yourself. Understanding what you want.

UNDERSTANDING YOURSELF

WHY ARE YOU UNHAPPY?

First think why you might be having the blues.

We have all heard about the well-known Monday blues. You've had a great weekend and then it's suddenly back to the grind. The grunge of routine. The clouds start to appear on your emotional horizon. 5 whole days of school or work stretch out ahead of you. This is usually the case if you don't like your work. Your choice of employment is critical to your happiness. If you cannot find any happiness, sense of self-worth or anything to look forward to from your work, you need to rethink your position in life. Make steps to change the situation. Look for other jobs. Start retraining or take up further training to get promoted or moved in your company. Do not jeopardise the job you have because being unemployed and penniless will certainly not bring a smile to anybody's face. But try to find somewhere that will give you some gratification. Even if it just has nicer offices, a place outside to sit at lunch or friendly team members to work with.

If this is not possible, try to find solace in the fact that you have a job. Being without income is certainly not a secure footing to start any journey to happiness. Be thankful for what you have. Life without a job may look a whole lot gloomier.

"Each day on this Earth is precious. Try not to squander any."

Other reasons you may be feeling sad:

- You let other people's problems become your problems. You let other people's bad moods become your bad moods. Living with a negative person can be extremely detrimental even to the most upbeat people. Be truthful to yourself and see if it is your partner who is giving you the blues always moaning about the weather, work and life. If they are, you need to blow their grey clouds away from you. Maybe they don't realise they are doing it, but you cannot allow their humdrum outlook on life to become your way of life.

- Another reason you may be feeling blue could simply be hormonal. We all run on cycles – that of women being far more broadcast and ridiculed than those of men – so give yourself a little leeway if it is your time to have a rest at being the go-getter or team mascot for everyone.

- If you have been hard on yourself, like working on a diet or slogging away at a project and not seen any rewards, that can also make you feel "down in the dumps".

You need to treat yourself with kid gloves in these circumstances. Be patient with yourself. Show a bit of understanding, just like you would to a friend. Treat yourself like your best friend. Maybe pep yourself up with some instantly gratifying goals like: finish painting that room or sorting out the patio or writing to Jack your long lost nephew. Once you complete these easy-to-achieve goals you will feel more driven. You will feel rewarded. That is an essential part of our psyche.

If you are hammering away at the same thing and not making progress – whether it's clinching a date with a girl/boy or trying to sell your latest invention – you might need to take stock of the situation. Try a new tact. Try a different line of attack. Try a different boy/girl!

- You might just be feeling lonely. Perhaps you haven't had human contact for a while, hiding as you do tucked away in your safe zone behind the curtains with your box sets. Or your loved one is miles away on business. Why not go see a friend? Or even get a cat or dog or hamster if you'd prefer something smaller. This sense of bonding will lift your spirits.

- Are you stuck like a broken record worrying about something... an exam, a presentation, the lack of money? Take a deep breath. You'll get through it. You will survive the event. Divert your thoughts through exercise, reading a comic, doing yoga. Do something outlandishly brave that is out of your comfort zone. Ski down from the top of a mountain, take a dive out of a plane, make friends with your neighbour who you fell out with 2 years ago – anything to get your blood pumping and refocus your thoughts away from your worries. Yes, a hair-raising experience is far more beneficial than worrying about lack of money or exams!

"Change is a great motivator and emotional redirector."

Rearrange your furniture, if you can't get away. A change is as good as a rest. Even if you are not into feng shui, think about your environment. Do you have nice things to look at? Is there anything pleasantly aesthetically pleasing about your living environment? If not, why not? Could you redecorate? Is your living space cluttered or drab? Get a throw, revamp. Buy a plant or two. This is easy to rectify and very uplifting.

<u>This is not called a **self**-help book by accident.</u>

There are so many ways you can help **yourself**.

- Changing your behaviour.
- Changing your habits.
- Changing your diet.
- Changing your routine.
- Changing your environment.

You may not be able to pinpoint exactly when or which change is helping you, but take it from me – they all help and they all make a difference... for the better.

"Today is yesterday's tomorrow."

You may already know this as you are wise - we cannot help but gain such pearls of wisdom as we get older!

"Like a snowball rolling into a snow boulder

We get wiser as we get older."

Today is the future you have been working towards.

Make today the day you want it to be.

Don't expect tomorrow or next year to be any different than today.

Cherish today. Cherish the here and now.

That is why all the yogi masters and meditation mentors are constantly encouraging their pupils to feel "grounded". It is not a bad connotation. Being "grounded" does not make you static; it is a process through which you feel connected with who you actually are, with what is happening around you **now**. If you cannot appreciate the present day you are living in or if you are constantly yearning for a better tomorrow, you will indeed miss the happy bus. You will constantly feel sad and miserable about yourself.

Learn to feel grounded. Learn to love today as yesterday's bright future.

<u>You have to hit the lows to hit the highs.</u>

I will touch on this more later in this book, but maintaining happiness on an even par consistently is nigh on impossible. It would be like keeping ten plates all spinning at the same speed all the time. Impossible. Sometimes the motors spinning your plates need to shutdown. Need to refuel. Being sad gives you a different perspective. It allows you to see things differently. This can actually be a positive help. It can help you evolve and become more creative, appreciative and grounded.

Let's not encourage your sadness though. Simply reap the potential. See the upside.

Was happiness a fad?
Or was it in the lost and found again behind the issues.
It might not be so bad,
We're all addicted to our tragedy,
I guess it's what it had to be
(Sum 41)

Accepting that you will have lows is different to becoming addicted to them or wallowing in your sadness. It is all too easy to be sad – hence the reference to it being an "addiction" – whereas happiness seems to be more transitory and short-term in our lives, like a "fad". Playing the victim or the hero in a "tragedy" might be appealing to some because it seems to be easier than working at succeeding and being happy. Well, it's not. Throw off your cloak of misery for it is weighing you down. Happiness through personal development, achievement and increased self-esteem is much more liberating and "easier" to live with than being addicted to sadness.

Maybe you cannot fully explain why you are sad or low. Perhaps it is easier for you to explain why you are *not happy*. This is a positive step in the right direction. Once you have opened up to yourself and faced why you are unhappy, you can build from this. Instead of combatting sadness front on, you are going to take it by surprise through the back door and go for the things that make you unhappy.

Examples of why you may not be happy:

- You have fallen out with someone you love and respect

- You don't feel love from your parent(s)

- You are not eating properly/how you want to

- You did not do as well as you expected in an exam or assessment

- You have let someone down

- You want to lose weight

- You hate your job or it's a dead-end job

- You want to quit a bad habit but can't

All these examples are "manageable" and may only be manifestations of a larger underlying problem you are ignoring. Say you are unhappy with your diet or fitness regime, it may be that you are actually sidestepping the real issue, which is a sense of failing in your past (a previous relationship, poor relationship with your mother/father, the loss of a friend). Dealing with "manageable" problems will help build your self-esteem. Each time you succeed in conquering a small area in your life you are becoming a more powerful warrior who will ultimately be able to defeat any major underlying problems causing sadness or lack of self-worth.

Major upsets in your life will naturally take time and may require professional help to heal, but the things you know to make you unhappy can be managed by you.

- You have fallen out with someone you love and respect

Solution: - You can make up or make amends with someone you love and respect

- You don't feel love from your parent(s)

Solution: - You can talk to your parent(s), start a conversation

- You are not eating properly/how you want to

Solution: - You can control your diet only buy what you want to eat, join a class or group

- You did not do as well as you expected in an exam or assessment

Solution: - You can re-sit your exam/assessment or take it as a sign to take a different path of learning

- You have let someone down

Solution: - You can apologise to someone you have let down

- You want to lose weight

Solution: - Join a gym. Make an inspiration board. You can lose weight (there are lots of helpful programs and groups)

- You hate your job or it's a dead-end job

Solution: - You can change jobs, retrain or learn to appreciate the fact you have a job

- You want to quit a bad habit but can't

Solution: - You can get help to quit a bad habit. Keep trying.

Other general solutions for removing negative emotions if you do not know exactly what is making you unhappy:

- You can self-heal through Reiki to unblock and let your Universal Life Energy flow through you again to take away the pain

- You can increase your happy hormone levels through exercise

- Take up meditation or Yoga to detox yourself from within and find a sense of calm

- Tell yourself 3 positive things every morning before you get out of bed. 3 things you like in life, that make you happy, that you are grateful for or proud of.

Understanding why you are unhappy is just as important as understanding what you want out of life – it helps you find your focus.

It helps you to decide what needs to be eliminated, this is the de-cluttering process. Remember the **O** and the **C** in **F-O-C-U-S**?

Offload the superfluous

Carry only what you need

As we go through life we pick up so much unwanted baggage. These can be in the forms of mistakes, bad habits, bad decisions, regrets and unwanted ties. Emotional and mental scarring. You need to offload the superfluous.

Bad habits like smoking, drinking or overeating can be offloaded more easily because it is within **your** power to do so. There is always plenty of help for anyone who wants to kick a habit. You just need to reach out and then accept the help.

Regrets may be a little harder to offload, but with time spent on making your life more positive, through self-healing, inward focus and striving for your goals, these regrets will soon be replaced with a new drive. You cannot change what has happened in your past, but you can change what is going to happen in your future – this is not written in stone.

Real-life example 1: You wish you'd never started to smoke. Stop!

I met a man aged 77. At 50 he was a heavy smoker and he was told he was going to loose his legs if he carried on smoking. He quit. Two decades later he is the John Travolta of the Salsa dance scene with his own classes, inspiring others to take up this beautiful form of artistic expression and movement. 77 and not in a wheelchair, 77 and moving around the dance floor with agility and grace, still inspiring people of all ages to join in with this uplifting and fun experience.

So quit. After just a few weeks and months you will feel better both physically and mentally.

Whatever is standing in your way of happiness can be knocked down.

Example 2: You hate your job. Change it! Retrain!

Firstly be thankful you have a job/income. Secondly if it is that bad, take the necessary measures to change it.

A middle-aged woman looking after 2 small children was sick of not seeing her children and doing a boring job in an office. She had a degree but nobody would employ her after she had taken a couple of years out for maternity. All her money was going to cover childcare and she didn't have a partner to support her. She started applying online as a freelance web content author. She did this after the children went to sleep and the chores were done. At first the work was slow, but then because her writing was so good, she was recommended on to other firms. Soon those couple of hours in the evening and on her lunch break weren't enough, she had to quit her job and now her sole income was from this freelance writing work. Her children then only went to nursery for a couple of hours a day to play with their friends, and she was able to manage her own hours and enjoy her family whilst building up her own business.

No excuses. Take hold of the reigns to your life.

As the wise skate punk band Sum 41 said (see quote above), don't leave your happiness in the in the "lost and found" for someone else to take, keep it with you, feed it, nurture it and enjoy it. Happiness cannot be cultivated or made to appear on cue, but we can stave off unhappiness by doing the things we like and by breaking through and dealing with the things that make us unhappy.

Most importantly when asking yourself why you are feeling low, BE HONEST WITH YOURSELF. Only then can you build the ladder to climb out of your hole.

Do not be afraid to take action. Do not be afraid of taking those first steps. Every day that passes leads to more stagnation. You are in charge of your destiny do not delay in starting to spin the wheel of your own good fortune.

CHAPTER 3   DEFINITION OF HAPPINESS

What does being happy mean to you?

The literal definition of happiness

> happiness 'hapɪnəs/ noun
>
> noun: happiness; plural noun: happinesses
>
> 1. the state of being happy.
>
> "she struggled to find happiness in her life"

Amazing isn't it that the example in the dictionary shows the antithesis of a constant state of happiness. It is a struggle. And yes it is a struggle for many people. I think a better example would have been: "A state of well-being accompanied by positive feelings and emotions." Anyway, I am in no position to re-write the dictionary!

Note: Happiness is not to be confused with euphoria, which is an even more transient state. Even more of an extreme. Euphoria tends to be more short-lived than the state of happiness. Instead of gliding on a feeling of happiness, we would be shooting up like rockets in a state of euphoria. Not a sustainable emotion.

> *Happiness is a mental or emotional state of well-being defined by*
>
> *positive or pleasant emotions ranging from contentment to intense joy.*

But then again, good old Wikipedia, whether you trust it or not, states both the extremes of simply being content and satisfied through to intense joy are encompassed under the single umbrella of "happy". This makes the whole feeling more of a sporadic, less consistent, i.e. harder to maintain as a constant throughout every day.

> *Happiness is a fuzzy concept.*
> *Related concepts are well-being,*
> *quality of life, flourishing, and*
> *contentment.*

(Source: Wikipedia, 2017)

Being happy doesn't seem to have its own "constant" essence. As already touched upon above, it is not an easy feeling to define into a nice tidy box. It is "fuzzy" – well done Wikipedia!

So perhaps a there is no clear-cut definition of happiness that we can add to our TO DO list and simply tick it off as being accomplished.

On an everyday list of things to do:

☑ Do the washing

☑ Take the kids to school

☑ Pay the tax man

☐ Be happy

☑ Mow the lawn

☑ Sew on Jack's buttons

☑ Finish tiling the bathroom

☑ Write birthday thank you notes

Or on our bucket list:

- ☑   Learn French
- ☑   Lose 10 lbs
- ☐   Be happy
- ☑   Go hand gliding
- ☑   Get a tattoo
- ☑   Walk on hot coals
- ☑   Go zorbing
- ☑   Be in a reality show

Being happy just isn't something you can tick off as being "done", it is an on-going state. Yes you may have experienced happiness and I hope you have. You may have experienced happiness numerous times. Now you want to ensure happiness is not a distant friend who you only see once in a blue moon.

I want to show you that happiness can be part of every day of your life.

I don't expect you to be doing an Irish jig every 5 minutes or to be singing at the top of your lungs for joy. No that is more akin to what society deems as madness than to what we are trying to achieve here.

I want you to lift yourself out of any slump, to lift your self-esteem. Find out why you feel down, why you don't jump out of bed every morning, because although I don't mean it literally, you should be "jumping out of bed" every morning. Every day you should be waking with a sense of contentment, butterflies in your stomach, looking forward to some part of your day, whether it is wearing a new piece of clothing, that free hour you know you'll get tonight to work on your go-kart or novel, that meet-up with friends, your next day to losing weight and gaining a great figure, that delicious meal you'll be cooking for your loved ones and who'll be singing your praises... the list of possible things to look forward to is endless.

Make sure every day has something in it that you like, that you want to do.

Here are some more ideas:

- Spending time with your child/children for an hour after work

- A good deed for your local church/charity like donating flowers, helping set up tables, carrying stuff

- A deluxe haircut/spa treatment that you have saved up for – maybe because you kicked a bad habit

- Half an hour playing with your cat/dog

- Skyping an old school friend/relatives abroad

- A cycle ride/walk through the woods

- Wearing a new outfit/shoes

- Playing the PlayStation/Xbox/Nintendo

- A lie-in

- A dance lesson

- Sitting out in your garden with a cold beer watching the sun set

- (add your own)

-

-

-

If you cannot think when you could possibly fit what you want to do in your day, maybe because you are too tired when you get home – try turning your day around. Play your console games in the morning, play with your kids in the morning... there is always a way. See what it is that is taking up your time other than work. You may be surprised to find a little 20-30 minutes for yourself is possible.

What does being happy mean to you?

Some people find having a tidy and clean home makes them happy, or rather they are not happy if it is messy and dirty.

This same rule of opposition can be applied to lots of situations:

"Happy when out in the free air on my bike" vs. "not as happy when I'm stuck indoors, not on my bike."

Some situations can be a bit more blurred in our minds

"Happy when my children are around but also happy when they are not."

Your own definition of happiness can be as "fuzzy" as the dictionary's or Wikipedia's definition. It's back to that old saying that the world is not black and white; it is filled with all sorts of shades of grey. People are capable of experiencing several emotions at once. Meaning it is possible for you to still remain optimistic even while you are being realistic:

"What it is"

It is madness

says reason

It is what it is

says love

It is unhappiness

says caution

It is nothing but pain

says fear

It has no future

says insight

It is what it is

says love

It is ridiculous

says pride

It is foolish

says caution

It is impossible

says experience

It is what it is

says love."

— Erich Fried, *Es ist was es ist. (It is what it is)* "

Just like this poem, things can be simple in life. It is impressive how the poet can be so simplistic and yet convey such an expressive message. Although there seems to be loss and futility at every turn, Erich Fried rather humorously conveys a sense of acceptance without any great burden or undue desperation.

That is how you should approach all the bad turns and dead ends that bring your happiness levels down: With a touch of humour and optimistic acceptance.

I have introduced a poem into this section of the guide because poetry can help us to explore our emotions. It does not have to be complex. We can find empathy in poetry, we can find solace and humour, intrigue and inspiration. Poetry satisfies both sides of our coin here: it can help us better understand ourselves and on the flip side it can lift our spirits.

I hope this will help you better understand what happiness means to you. To look at things objectively, not so black and white. It is not clear-cut. Nonetheless certain actions and thoughts give us a warm feeling inside. What makes you happy may be insignificant to others or be something they hate – like volunteer work or helping a neighbour. Whatever it is that makes you feel good about yourself, feel better about your day, does not have to fit into any conventional box with a smiley face on the outside. It can be anything that gives you a smiley face on the inside of you.

Remember the **U** in **FOCUS**?

Understand yourself

You can best help yourself once you understand what you want.

You may not be able to decide this as easily as you think. As we move through life our views change, what we may have wanted as a teenager may no longer apply or be possible. The best advice I can give you is to be honest with yourself. Do not be afraid of what you want out of life. You only have one shot at this. It is never to late to make a change.

By reading this book you are already taking a step towards changing. And all those thoughts that lead you to purchasing this book have been fuelled with emotion and a desire for change. You've already done the hard part and recognised you need change in your life. Now all you need to do is whittle away the superfluous and concentrate on what you want. What will make you and ultimately those around you happy? Because happiness, like laughter and smiling is infectious. Your happiness will spread just like your sadness did.

I say this to balance the scales. You may feel that doing what you want is selfish, but in essence others around you will benefit and they will respect you more for it.

Ask yourself what you want. Once you have grasped this, it is advisable to create time for these moments every day. Moments to reassert your goals and focus, moments to take steps to achieving those goals.

Don't forget: Today is when your tomorrow starts.

CHAPTER 4   MOTIVATION

10 pick-me-ups for when you are down.

10 things that'll pick you up when you're down

MOTIVATION FACTORS

1. Music

2. Your achievements

3. Competition

4. Pets

5. A friendly ear

6. Love

7. Family

8. Exercise

9. Not getting angry

10. Doing a good deed

As you may notice not all drivers are solitary activities. There is a reason for this. Loneliness is a main contributor to depression, mental health problems.[1] Let's look at them all in more depth:

1. Music

Whether you listen to it, sing, play an instrument or even dance to it, music is such a transporter of emotions. Even if you listen to the sad songs it can make you feel better about yourself in a poetic romantic way. You can still find your inner peace with an emotive piece from Bach or one of Adele's many songs of rejection.

Music gives you a surge, like a electric shock to your emotions, its effects get right in there. You have no defence barriers. You don't want any either, just flow with the emotions of the music. It will change your state of mind. Playing an instrument or singing is an even stronger medium for transporting your emotions as you are physically involved. Releasing your grief through singing (or shouting!) is very "medicinal". In meditation the vibrations of our vocal actions on our organs have been found to be extremely beneficial and can qualm a lot of anguish and give us relief. On a physical level, singing increases your oxygen intake

[1] It's long been known that elderly people are more prone to depression and other mental-health problems if they live on their own. New research suggests the same pattern may also be found in younger, working-age adults.

In a study of nearly 3,500 men and women ages 30 to 65, researchers in Finland found that people who lived alone were more likely that their peers to receive a prescription for antidepressant drugs. One quarter of people living alone filled an antidepressant prescription during the seven-year study, compared to just 16% of those who lived with spouses, family, or roommates.

"Living alone may be considered a mental-health risk factor," says lead author Laura Pulkki-Råback, Ph.D., a lecturer at the University of Helsinki's Institute of Behavioral Sciences. The study was published in the journal BMC Public Health. (Source: CNN)

making your blood pump faster, stimulating the brain. Depending on how loud you sing, you can also "drown out" all that negative nagging in your head, releasing your emotional blockages. That is why you cry sometimes when you sing a touching or moving song. It's a great release and a metaphysical form of transportation to our moods.

2. Your achievements

This motivation factor is a little bit more sensitive. You may feel that you have not achieved what you want in life. Bear in mind where you are in life: too young to have achieved, too busy to have achieved, feel it's too late to achieve... if you follow some of my advice (not just in this book but my other self-help books, or those of other worthy "guides") you will be able to look at your list of achievements and feel a sense of satisfaction. That satisfaction gets you one step closer to feeling happy and one step further away from feeling sad.

We all criticise our own abilities far more than others. We are our harshest judge. When you are feeling low, remind yourself of just what you have achieved in life and what you are taking measures to achieve next and you may just turn the corner onto "I'm Okay Street".

Your achievements can be personal (e.g. giving up a habit, saving money, loosing weight, etc.); they can be non-materialistic (e.g. helping a friend in need, volunteering for charity or school, etc.) or getting through a difficult period (e.g. a death, a divorce, an illness, etc.).

What I have achieved list – what does your look like?

It doesn't have to be over-the-top:

- — Set up multi-million dollar incorporation
- — Saved thousands of lives
- — Won Olympic gold

It can be much simpler:

- Helped an old man cross the road
- Saw my baby's first smile
- Gave up my seat for a pregnant lady
- Did my first set of 100 sit-ups
- Opened the door for someone
- Let someone skip the queue who was in a rush
- Made someone happy
- Kept to my fitness regime for 3 months
- Wrote the outline to my book
- Published my first book
- Kept a roof over my family's head for 10 years
- Stopped smoking for a whole year
- Lost 2 lbs.

An achievement doesn't have to be becoming the champion of some sport or discipline, it can be something personal. Don't be too hard on yourself. Every achievement is a step in the right direction. A building block to happiness.

3. Competition

This may not seem like an obvious "pick-me up". I also do not recommend that you "compare" yourself to others, because all that glitters is not gold and what may seem like a happy couple, the perfect family or an ideal role model may in fact turn out to be just a successful front.

I am referring to a "healthy" form of competitiveness.

Seeking competition whether at work or in your private life can help spur you on to become an even better version of yourself. Stagnation can bring on a sense of disenchantment with life. Never wallow. That does not take you to "I'm Okay Street", it takes you to "No Drive". By actively competing with your piers or superiors, you are encouraged to excel, to stretching yourself further than you normally would. Going beyond what you think are your natural boundaries is a real exhilaration. You can wow yourself. It's amazing how this can pick you up and make you happier.

Seek stimulation from your surroundings at work, in your club and among associates. This motivation will light your fire and pull you away from feeling disengaged and low. Incentivise yourself through competing with others. Working as part of a team can be extremely beneficial: "Working together and helping each other releases brain chemicals that enhance motivation, pleasure, and bonding." Marilee B. Sprenger, author of *The Leadership Brain for Dummies*. "The brain strongly desires these feel-good chemicals..."

From this "competition" and "feel-good" factor comes increased creativity, productivity and innovation – all of which are highly rewarding and will assure more happiness in your day and greater self-esteem – one of the holy grails of happiness.

4. Pets

This may not be to everyone's liking but if you love animals it can be extremely rewarding. The pure love you receive from a canine or feline companion can be very comforting. Even smaller pets such as gerbils, hamsters or birds lend this same sense of gratification. Looking after them, seeing them thrive, feeling their affection is a sure way to keep those blues away. Pets ask for nothing in return (a safe home, food and perhaps a few creature comforts), but they give so much.

Here's a quick overview of their benefits:

They make us more active. Owning a cat or dog can lower high levels of cholesterol and triglycerides, according to the Centers for Disease Control and Prevention (CDC).

They help us develop empathy

They raise our self-esteem through unconditional love and a boost to our well-being

Pets lower stress and depression

Stroking your cat or dog can lower your blood pressure and make you feel calmer. Even watching fish can ease tense muscles.

Playing with your pet increases the levels of the feel-good chemicals serotonin and dopamine in your brain. A study conducted by the National Institutes of Health (NIH) found that people recover from a stressful situation more quickly when they're with their pets than with their partners or friends.

Pets connect you to a community

Pets get you moving[2]

Pets will brighten up your day. They are free from the stresses of human life, they remind us of what it is to simply live and enjoy the simple things – a bit like children. Even more rewarding is when you give a pet without a home a new chance in life. This ranks high on the gratification bar.

I'm sure you will also have heard the studies stating that stroking your pets can help to ease stress and bring a sense of calm. What a wonderful gift.

---

[2] Source: Esther Crain and www. humana.com

5. A friendly ear

You've no doubt heard of the saying: "A problem shared is a problem halved." As I will explore in more depth in Chapter 6, just by airing your problem, complaint or worry, talking it out with someone who has a vested interested in you, like a friend, someone at work who knows the situation, a member of your family, even a professional, can instantly alleviate your angst.

In a further step, this third party can bring new insight to your problem or offer you comfort as a minimum – a really important "minimum" not to be sniffed at.

As just one person you cannot see all angles of a situation – though you may think you do. Someone else may be able to offer a solution you had not thought of or simply be there to help you through the rough times – and you can be there for him or her in his or her tough times too.

This comfort or pulling yourself out of what may seem to you like a dead end will help you to combat the feelings of negativity and engender that all-important emotion called "hope".

With hope you can start down the road to happiness once more.

6. Love

Ah love!

If you're ever so lucky as to be in love or to have someone who loves you, then you should never be unhappy. Love, in its truest sense, is non-judgmental and selfless. The person who loves you will give you so much to enjoy in life, so much to look forward to. They will brighten your days and lift your self-esteem – not as a deliberate act, simply by loving you for who you are and the things you do.

Open your doors to love, do not live as a recluse. You are allowed to feel happy and in love.

(NB: Enjoy it for as long as it lasts and make no demands of it. Let love take its course). You don't have to be lonely. Loneliness will not help you find happiness.

7. Family

Family is a bit like Marmite – you either love it or you hate it.

We do not get to choose our family. This means you may get dealt a really bad hand, an okay hand or a great hand. No matter which one it is, your family is also you. You are part of a family. If someone like a brother or cousin comes to you, there is already a natural affinity, something in common. This may help in times of need.

The family members you are fortunate enough to get along with are like cushions. They are there for you.

I don't know what I would have done without my brother and sister-in-law. They have seen me through so many sticky and sometimes sad situations. They don't have to offer physical or monetary help, they can simply be there in the back of your mind as a form of mental support. When you know you are not alone, everything seems so much more manageable, less daunting.

Use your cushion or cushions.

8. Exercise

"Oh no!" I hear some of you cry, "Don't make me jog! I am reading this book to be happy not tortured." Don't fear my fellow travellers of life, I will not make you jog. But I will suggest a few jumps for joy.

It may be the last thing you feel like doing but just do it anyway.

Jump up and shout YES. Raise your hands in the air. Jump! YES!

Do this 15 to 20 times. When you have overcome your shyness, you can even add I'M GREAT to your next of 20 and then I LOVE LIFE to the next set and so on.

The positive vocal reaffirmation helps what is happening physically to your body.

I did not have to look too hard when researching the scientific based impact of exercise with regards to generating a more positive outlook on life. The Internet and our libraries are literally flooded with information promoting the benefits of exercise in terms of positivity and improving attitudes. Now all you have to do is ignore your "naughty" you who is telling you to stay in bed or watch a movie instead of grabbing your bike or grabbing your running shoes and getting out there for 20 minutes. Don't think. Just go. Once you are out there you'll want more, you'll love it. You'll come back home in a completely different frame of mind.

Yes, happiness is just minutes away – literally:

Serotonin and dopamine are chemicals produced in the brain -- neurotransmitters -- that improve mood and protect against mental health disorders. Serotonin, which is produced by long-term cardio exercise, decreases depression and hostility, and improves agreeable social behaviour. Dopamine improves your mood and long-term memory. It stimulates highly pleasurable feelings in the brain and could contribute to what is called "runners high."[3]

Exercising can also help you release a lot of pent up energy, negative energy, which leads us nicely onto the next motivational tip:

9. Not getting angry

Easier said than done right?

But all those negative emotions you release when you are angry can leave you feeling depleted and it only brings more negativity to the situation.

Anger fuels a fire, it does not extinguish it.

I you think back on your past angry moments, you'll see that they never bought about anything positive. This is not a recommendation for suppressing anger and to let I build up inside so you can explode like a volcano for no reason – like maybe the cat is sitting in your chair and you hurl abuse at your spouse! No, the idea is not to get angry in the first place. See the situation for what it is. Don't stress about it, don't jump around and shout. You don't achieve anything but your own demise like Rumpelstiltskin – and I don't mean to patronise you, but fairy tales have always had a deeper meaning, designed to teach our children from a young age to be better people. Anger does not lead to happiness.

Remaining calm will help you to dissipate the situation to make a better

---

[3] www.livestrong.com

decision, not to react quickly and so or do something you might regret.

All these actions will lead to a better outcome. Not falling prey to the anger will avoid a sad and hurtful outcome. You will also avoid that acidic rise in your stomach leaving you full of regret and even more stress.

This is not about bottling up anger so you can explode at a later date for what appears to be no reason at all, it is about seeing all sides of a situation and taking your time to react. Be responsive instead of reactive. Tame your inner fire-breathing dragon!

10. Doing a good deed

You don't have to go and cook for your elderly neighbour every night or think of this as a chore, it could be as simple as sharing a positive message on your social media network or blog. Connecting with people in this way, by praising or thanking them will not only make others feel good, but it will reinforce you to have a more positive routine.

By having a positive routine and nurturing your relationships with people around you will close the door to negative thinking.

Try it every morning or evening and see what a positive impact it will have on your life.

Looking for the good and the positive you can do in life squeezes out the negative.

Naturally if you would like to engage in more "good-deeds" such as working in the soup kitchens, volunteering at a charity or other social acts of kindness, you will be ramping up those "happy points". People working together out of the kindness of their heart engender a positive atmosphere. You will gain positivity yourself from these social connections and constructive atmospheres.

There are of course more motivational factors, some of which I mention in my concluding chapter, however these 10 are a good start to add to your daily routine (even just one or two!) to boost your happiness factor.

CHAPTER 5   THE ELITE CLUB

Ridiculously happy members only.
How society conditions us.

Being happy and staying happy is only privy to the few members of the Elite Club.

Don't be fooled into this way of thinking. We may not be entitled to a lot things in life due to where we are born or the restrictions placed on us by society, but there is nothing Un-entitling you to being happy. I would say being happy is one of life's basic prerequisites.

To quote R. Kipling's *Jungle Book* it is one of the "Bare necessities of life".

We see mentions of happiness everywhere in art:

"We will all be happy at some stage…. Won't we?"

This paean to the inevitability of happiness was inspired by a giant text installation (of the same name) by the artist Ugo Rondinone.

Or alternatively:

"The Dog Days Are Over"
Happiness hit her like a train on a track
Coming towards her stuck still no turning back
Happiness hit her like a bullet in the back

The lyrics to the song itself convey a sense of moving on to a new chapter in life, and getting away from unhappier times in the past.

"Run fast for your mother, run fast for your father
Run for your children, for your sisters and brothers
Leave all your love and your longing behind
You can't carry it with you if you want to survive"

Florence and the Machine

The reason happiness features so heavily in art is because it is one of the major emotions in life. One of the inspirational motivators along with hate, revenge, desire, revenge, passion and jealousy.

Happiness cannot be ignored. Or rather, it should not be ignored.

Doing what you want is an essential factor in being happy. Just like on the flip side of the same coin, doing what you don't want to do is a sure fired way of being unhappy.

Unfortunately, sometimes art, in the form of films, celebrities and social media, can skew the interpretation of happiness. Giving individuals the false impression of what they need to be happy. Movies are transitory, the lives of celebrities as they are conveyed through social media are superficial. Because we don't want to see or know about their failings, we want them to be our idols and modern gods. Not simply different versions of us.

The happiness you see on social media, in films and even in some books is not real. It is not reality. Art is not reality. It is an interpretation of reality.

Any form of fiction is a snippet, reflection or allegorical depiction of a situation. It is not a continuous sequence of events. Real life is a continuous sequence of events. It does not stop.

Real life is not framed, caricatured or encased in a limited format. Therefore it would be a mistake to compare your life with any such artificial depictions.

Keep it real.

People who don't keep it real end up being addicted to a drug or TV series or some kind of fantasy to break up their reality. Embrace reality. Make your reality a superlative of any artificial recreation. Be the film, be the book, be the story.

Just like other addictions, these "addictions" to TV and films are something you can control, e.g. the odd drink, the odd couch potato session, then there is nothing wrong with having a little time out from the routine – only if *it* doesn't control *you*. Balance is key here.

We are watching more and more films. Living the life of others rather than our own. Whether it's reality TV, talent shows or box set series.

We are watching life through the life of others. These are not our own experiences.

So how are we supposed to be ready to feel or understand our own reactions when what we are experiencing so much of the time is passive?

We can't.

Surely we are becoming programmed on how to react because we have been virtually living in somebody else's skin for weeks and weeks. TV is a form of voluntary brainwashing.

We are distancing ourselves away from our own self, our own emotions. We are not giving ourselves the chance to grow into our own individual personality.

The more we watch from a young age, and let's be honest, it is getting younger and younger, the more inept we and future generations will be at understanding our own wants, needs and reactions. The latter is simply a product of the first two, because we will be imitating the feelings of others – almost like robots and so these consequential reactions will not be our own.

This trend is extremely dangerous. When left to our own devices, when faced with big decisions we will have nothing or very little to fall back on because we have been filled with the false lives of reality TV and made-up characters.

As I stated in Chapter 2, it is essential to know what you want. To know what drives you. And just as important in finding happiness, it is important to understand and recognise what you **do not want** in your life.

The first factor of what you want will drive you through life.

It will be the driving force behind all your decisions. Even as basic as: Do I want a career or do I want a family more? Do I want a dog? Do I want to buy more pretty clothes? Do I want a recognised qualification? Do I want to live in a different country? Do I want polished shoes?

If you know the answers to the questions and you know the questions to be asked, you can feel happy and fulfilled when you have achieved them. If you do not know yourself, you cannot even start down this path, let alone get to the end where you feel happy or a sense of happiness for having achieved what you wanted.

Once we have achieved our goals, we then move on to the realms of never having enough and always wanting more. This is not a "risk", it is only natural and it is healthy if you manage to appreciate and feel gratitude for what you have achieved and what you have.

This is the sense of being "grounded" and grateful. There is nothing wrong with achieving your goals and then moving on to achieving more. What would be wrong is to accept stagnation. It is not a natural state of mind. Stagnation leads to more unhappiness.

Let's steer back to the detrimental influence of TV and social media. The extremes that we are filling our heads and minds and hearts with.

Nobody wants to watch a film or a series where everyone is content and happy. How boring. We want action. Sudden tragic loss. A frightening surprise. Exhilarating love affairs.

Romantic encounters. Thrills and spills. We are filling ourselves with extremes and we cannot live on extremes in our everyday lives. That just doesn't happen.

In our everyday lives we have routine, repetitions, mundane chores like washing, dressing and cooking. Not necessarily in that order, but you must agree that would be a dull film.

So how do we overcome this? How do we differentiate reality from fiction? A series of extremes with our sometimes mundane lives.

If you are the hero in your story, you will end every day with a smile knowing you were the best you could be that day.

Even if you I achieved very little in material terms. You do not need to "achieve" just for the sake of it. If you try and force it, you get frustrated and depressed. Instead use the power you have on days when you feel "energised" and it just pours out of you.

Each day has to be a day filled with stuff you like, devoid of stuff you don't like and one step towards achieving your dream or dreams.

Otherwise what is the point of being alive?

What's the point of being you? You might as well be a cardboard cut-out of a soap opera queen or Vlogger.

Modern society is stressful though and it does seem like there is an Elite Club where the exclusive members list alone is allowed to be happy in this world.

Here's an example of the unnecessary stresses:

Oh my god I haven't done my 30 minutes of yoga today. Argh what will I do – my world is falling apart!!

This is a perfect example of how hypocritical our modern-day society is.

Yoga is supposed to be relaxing and suddenly it is turned into a stress factor if you have not managed to fit it into your daily routine. Society pushes us to achieve, to tick those must-dos in a day such as:

- work like a maniac more than every other maniac

- get facial treatment to make you look younger

- do your "workout 'til I drop" routine

- be the perfect mother/father

- be a go-getter

- get into work before everyone else and leave after everyone else has left

- squeeze in a relaxing yoga routine... which then isn't relaxing because it becomes a chore.

Stop modelling your life on soap operas and box sets.

You are not supposed to be working non-stop for 8, 10 or 12 hours a day.

Remember the **S** in **FOCUS**?

Stop worrying

People spend so much time worrying about what they are supposed to be doing because society (certainly Western society) has conditioned them to be constant go-getters, mega-rich, successful or you are a failure. Stop worrying. Don't compare yourself.

If you have what YOU want, then it doesn't matter if you don't have the Barbie Body or the holiday home in Bermuda. You may want to live in a hut and travel the world. You define your own happiness remember. Let the media do the worrying about how they are going to keep making great films without rehashing all the old stuff and how they are going to keep the celebrities bright, shiny and tummy-tucked for generations to come.

Your role is to reset your internal compass. Get back onto YOUR track. It's the easiest and best way to be. You simply need to:

BE YOU

KNOW YOU

NURTURE YOU

CHAPTER 6   BE A PART NOT APART

The loneliness factor and asking for help

Being on your own can really get you down.

If you are in a serious situation where perhaps your partner does not allow you to socialise or see your friends and family, call for professional help – call for help anywhere you can. Don't wait. Your life is too short to be taken away from you.

If your isolation is self-inflicted, take steps to change this. Go out, join a club, even if it is the local bingo club, a charity, dance club, political party group... get out of the house, help in the children's after-school clubs, scouts, anything where you are part of a team.

You could choose a club where you all have a common goal and are like-minded, e.g. a writer's club or football club, or you could join a group with people that are different to you and of all ages, e.g. self-defence classes or environmental groups. Meeting different people with different beliefs and backgrounds but a common interest will help you grow and diversify – and forget your sadness.

This is especially applicable if you don't or aren't able to work, or if you are raising children on your own. You can get lonely otherwise.

Never feel that relying on other people is a weakness.

You can be the FRIENDLY EAR:

You are just as helpful to them: Listen to what they have to say; do not just use others as soundboards for your depression, regrets, mistakes.

When you listen you may find that

- you can help them to, ease their burden

- offer solutions

- find new ways to be happy and help yourself and family/loved ones

- forget about your problems; find out their funny stories

- realise they have it much worse than you!

As I say in all my books **YOU ARE IN CHARGE!**

Don't wait for someone else to come and make your life better. You have to do it. It is your life. Others will help you. People are a lot kinder than they are sometimes portrayed. But you have to go and seek help. You have to share and communicate. You cannot expect your partner, family or friends to simply understand what is going on in your head and heart. You have to explain it to them. You approach them. Sometimes you may only need to open up a little, sometimes you may need to explain a lot more, but in the end I guarantee you will feel a lightening of your spirit once you have started to share your thoughts and feelings.

People are not mind readers. You have to share a little in order to receive. Have you ever been there to help someone else?

Real-life example – asking for help:

A single mother for 13 years who is very protective of her sons. She is very independent. She finds it hard to ask for help because she has done everything herself. Every decision from the brand of toothpaste she buys to which mortgage package she chooses. She does it all on her own. So when she faced major problems with her 16-year-old son and his teenage attitude grew like a scary Goliath, she was at a loss as to what to do. He simply was not listening to her anymore (sound familiar?). He was hearing the same voice, hers, the same lines, and nothing was changing. The details are irrelevant, however, the steps she took to remedy a situation she could not change on her own after trying for almost a year are very relevant.

She called out for help.

She reached out to the last person we might have thought she would ever reach out to – yes, you guessed it, her ex-husband. Although they had been on amicable terms for over a decade, they had never let their lives merge in a personal way.

She explained what his son was going through. She told him she needed his help. She asked him for his help.

And do you know what happened? 2 really big things happened.

Well I won't keep you in anticipation for THE big one: he said yes, of course he would help.

But THE really big surprise to me was that as soon as she had asked for his help she said she felt a tremendous sense of alleviation.

By sharing her dilemma, her grief and troubles with someone who cared she felt all the burdens of the past year lift away like boulders on the wings of angels being transported far away and vanishing.

The outcome I am pleased to say was equally positive, but not without its own obstacles. Simply by having someone to share the bumpy ride with, to talk about the obstacles, how to circumnavigate them, how to tackle them had been enough to lift her out of her state of despair and be stronger to help her son and they dealt with his problems together.

Perhaps you are in a similar state of despair where you feel you are dealing with insurmountable problems all on your own or you are feeling trapped by a situation you don't see a way out of.

Call for help.

As an individual you can only see a finite number of solutions. Others may see a way out of your dilemma that perhaps you can't.

Who you call on depends on your circumstances. It may be a close friend, someone you haven't seen for years or perhaps an organisation. Most people are always eager to help. The only thing stopping this flow of help is our inability to ask for it.

Naturally, once you have torn down the walls of your restricting situation or conflict, you are then more able to stand on your own two feet. The person who helps you break through the threshold to the other side of your gloom is merely the gatekeeper, you will then find your strength again and be able to continue on your own, with only the need of the odd prop up here and there. (You do not want to become a drain on those who help you, so don't.)

If there is hurt in your past, you need to move on.

Do not dwell on the past, do not play back your life in your head over and over again showing all the things you would have done differently.

If you do this you will be miserable and stuck in the past. If your mind is in the past, so are your actions and emotions. You will not be able to be a part of the present or the future.

Start thinking about what you want from the future, for your children and yourself. This will bring about changes in your life. Remember: FOCUS. Aim for where you want to go.

Perhaps introduce yoga or Reiki or meditation into your life, even if it is something you have never done before: If you want change in your life, if you want movement, start things moving. Start to release the past so you can enjoy the present and get on with the future.

A bit of a simple analogy I suppose is the idea of legs and movement, but it is decidedly poignant and true. When you are moving forwards both on a physical and emotional level you propel yourself forwards and your life forwards.

Think about what you have and what you want for tomorrow.

Pull yourself out of past regrets otherwise you'll become entrenched. The quagmire of yesterday's mistakes will keep you stuck in the past.

Your hope and dreams for tomorrow will release you from these bonds, liberate you from these heavy ties.

Move forward to want you want by taking charge of your life, instead of blaming the past or blaming others or blaming your situation.

Break these chains and allow yourself to live the life you want. You can start making steps towards what you want in your life. This could be as simple as redecorating your house or garden, buying the outfit you've always wanted, getting that hair cut or colour you never dared, something you want, to really big stuff like getting the job you want, giving up work and travelling, breaking way from a bad relationship, stopping a bad habit or addiction that is dominating your life.

Once you are free of these shackles you will feel a lightening within. You will be happy to wake up in the morning instead of fearing the day.

Embrace the help you will receive from others. Just like you would readily help anyone in need, others are there to do the same for you – expecting nothing in return.

Although I mention society in my guide as a malevolent force with its false doctrines on being perfect and the superficial unsustainable American Dream, there is a part to society that embraces its fellow man and woman. Society at this micro level is extremely supportive. Being part of a club or a social group, visiting your neighbours or making time for your family and friends can distract you from your sense of loneliness and help you realise you are not alone. You do not have to fight this battle alone.

Being a part of something is extremely rewarding and motivational. Others can spur you on to becoming something you never even dreamed of yourself.

What would you like to be a part of?

Go on, give it a try. Be a part and not apart.

CHAPTER 7   THE FUTURE

Make it bright. Make it yours.

It's your future: Plan things to look forward to. That's the easy remedy: Trips, breaks away, a hot bath and pamper night, a new course/class, buying a new car or new shoes, joining a club – it's your choice.

Remember what we covered in Chapter 1– understand what you want. Once you know this you can plan things that you will look forward to. You may reward yourself after saving up or find "free" ways to brighten your days e.g. planning a get-together with friends, skyping your family, take up a creative hobby, learn how to dance or going for a walk to have some time out.

You must have things to look forward to. Think of your list now and set out which you can do, which ones you have to save for and prioritise. Set some manageable goals first and then the more expensive ones for later – you don't want to bring negativity on yourself by overspending!

Going back to go forwards:

Easy as 1-2-3

Let's look back at other areas you have covered with the help of this guide before moving forwards.

1. Understanding yourself. Understand why you are feeling low.

- It may just be in your "cycle". You need some downtime to regroup and recharge. Even machines cannot sustain racing around at 100 miles per hour. They need to stop and refuel.

- It may be someone close to you that you let down or that let you down. Communicate, open up the dialogue.

- You feel like an under-achiever. Make sure it is your standards you are living to and not those set by others/society.

2. Look back on your achievements list. Take courage from it. Boost your self-confidence yourself, don't always wait for others to do this. They are busy with their own lives, their own problems.

3. Look at the 10 motivational tips (add your own) and goad yourself into a positive state of mind. Retrain that naughty brain of yours and be positive. Use Reiki, yoga or meditation to unblock deep-rooted sorrow.

As you get older (and perhaps more mature!) you will realise that life slows down. Everything is not as fast-paced as when you were a teenager. Not every day is a lifetime and you realise you will not be the next James Dean: Live fast. Die young. Instead you need to take everything one step at a time. Split your day into manageable "chunks":

- Time for work
- Time for household chores
- Time for the family
- Time for you
- Time for learning
- Time for achieving
- Downtime

Don't feel like you have to rush. Happiness, if it is to be sustained, cannot be rushed. Yes, there are a few activities that can instantly lift you, such as exercise or doing a good deed, but after looking at the "definition of happiness" in Chapter 2, I hope you understand that happiness can be a permanent state of mind. It does not have to be sporadic. It replaces the constant negative state of mind you may have been in before reading this guide.

You can easily train yourself to be consistently sad, by repeating the following over and over:

- I hate my job

- I've done nothing with my life

- What's the point?

- I just want to watch TV

- I deserve another drink/smoke

- There's no way I can afford that holiday/house

- I'm useless

Perhaps that is what you have. You dwell on the negative. Mull over mistakes and regrets, live in the past.

Now it's time to retrain yourself to being consistently happy – with peaks of euphoria and moments of stillness and reflectiveness by repeating:

- I can do this

- I want to change

- My goals are within my reach

- I am grateful for what I have

- I can build on what I have

- Step by step – no big deal

- Today is the start of the future I want

- I am not alone

Like I said earlier, you cannot be expected to be jumping for joy all the time. You are allowed to have downtime but save your sadness not for self-pity, but for moments that truly require grief.

Remember, don't be hard on yourself. Do not make unjust demands of yourself. If you are not in the right frame of mind you will most likely spend endless hours hammering away at the same idea, drawing, story, etc. and achieve nothing other than frustration. You can either wait, or put yourself in the right frame of mind. It is up to you to understand yourself using the advice above. Are you in a different cycle or are you just feeding yourself excuses?

I hope you understand how important it is to go through these steps one by one.

You must understand yourself. In doing so you will understand your limits. Know when to push yourself. When to take a day or week off. But not a holiday from life! When to feel proud about yourself. Not to be too hard on yourself.

You then move on to understanding what happiness means to you. If it is living a stress-free life or being a go-getter and achieving high goals, at least you'll understand your parameters.

Once you find understanding of yourself and what makes you happy, then you can avoid those phases of low self-esteem. And always remember IT IS WHAT YOU WANT NOT WHAT SOCIETY TELLS YOU that is important in finding happiness (please note I am not condoning breaking the law!).

Make your goals achievable to **avoid disappointment**.

All too often we hear the phrases: "make every day count", "live each day as though it were your last", while these are worth pondering on, you still need to take a **BALANCED APPROACH**. You do not need to react in an extreme manner.

Take time out. For whatever reason we have been given time on this earth. You are allowed to have the odd lazy day and squander some time on fruitless activities. That is all part of living. As the Italians say – "la dolce vita". So take time over eating a delicious meal, take time on your days off to do nothing. Don't burn yourself out working, cleaning or worrying.

If a person wants to be the next best bodybuilder they cannot go full steam ahead and lift 100kg. They have to gradually build up their body. Start with less weight. Focus on eating the right foods. Make sure they stretch and alternate their routines.

If they just go gung-ho without building up a foundation first - the building blocks - they risk (and it is a high risk) injuring themselves, torn ligaments, sprains, etc. and the damage may put a full stop to their dreams.

Take things one step at a time.

More tips for your future routine of positivity

1. Add a ray of sunshine to your day:

"Are you suffering from depression and fatigue during winter time? Winter depression can have many causes, but vitamin D deficiency may be the culprit. Human beings are dependent on the Sun in many ways; we cannot survive without its light and warmth. The Sun's movement regulates our circadian rhythm, which impacts various hormones in the body including serotonin (happiness), melatonin (sleepiness), and vitamin D.

When we don't get enough sunshine, especially in the winter, we can develop winter depression, also called SAD (Seasonal Affective Disorder), which effects at least 1 in 5 Americans, more women than men. According to research, SAD can be improved with vitamin D supplementation."[4]

Doing it the natural way is obviously best. Otherwise you can supplement with tablets. It doesn't have to be every day because your body stores it, but try to squeeze in 10 minutes to half an hour every day. The outdoors does wonders to lift our spirits.

2. Brain break

Other activities that can help you distress by refocusing your mind will also be helpful in tearing down that wall of anxiety and sadness. You can read, listen to music (as mentioned above), go for a walk (a change of scenery), get involved in a creative hobby, meditate, have a massage – these are not cover-up gimmicks, these activities will actually reduce

---

[4] Source: www.healthyhappynwise.com

your levels of worry and help restore balance in your mind so that you can FOCUS on what is important after giving your brain a break

3. Building blocks

You need to build yourself back up again.

Again, this is all subjective. It depends on how low you are feeling. The building block theory needs to be adapted to suit your personal circumstances.

If you have hit the worst of lows as a result of the death of loved one, learning of devastating news you always felt only happened to others or losing your job – just a s a few examples – you must bear in mind one key fact.

It is not your fault.

There are aspects of life beyond your influence

Although this may not bring you the comfort you need, it will provide with a platform for your sanity. For your ability to keep a level head in the days ahead. You do not need to burden yourself with feelings of frustration. You need to be strong for yourself and those around you.

4. Slow down

Sometimes we fill our lives with endless tasks, duties and pursuits to fill the void inside, to fill our time so we do not have to think about what we do not want to think about – so we do not have time or energy to face what is actually making us sad.

It takes a brave person to stop. Someone who knows their parameters or is willing to learn them.

Slow down. Listen to yourself. If need be talk with a close friend. Let it all come pouring out. In words. In tears. In anger.

Do this for as many times as you need to. Until you feel depleted. The depletion is you getting rid of all your negative feelings. You are now ready to fill yourself again with positivity. You have to wipe the slate clean and then soar from the ashes like the phoenix.

You are allowed to have slow moments and pensive moments, don't misunderstand this goal of sustaining your happiness as being a persistent form of euphoria. Extremes cannot be maintained for once they are they become the norm and new extremes are formed. The happiness I wish for you and all those living on this beautiful planet is that sense of self-worth, feeling great to be you and yes, a little chirpy just about being alive.

Staying happy is the best drive for your own motivation in your personal or entrepreneurial pursuits.

Summary

TOP TIPS

In an emergency if you're feeling really low:

PUT MUSIC ON – it has to be loud

GO EXERCISE: run, swim, skip, jump, anything!

GO SEE A FRIEND (not text, not phone) SEE THEM (skype if they are miles away)

LOOK AT YOUR "What I have achieved list"

SING LOUDLY

CREATE A "Something to look forward to list"

HAVE FAITH IN YOUR CONVICTIONS

FOLLOW YOUR GUT INSTINCT

DO NOT WALLOW IN SELF-PITY

YOU ARE NOT ALONE

RID YOURSELF OF NEGATIVITY

SURROUND YOURSELF WITH POSITIVE PEOPLE

There is no start and end to making happiness a consistent part of your life - it is an on-going process. Happiness is infinite.

Nobody knows how it feels to be you apart from you.

Make sure you tuned into the ME channel. Never lose sight of yourself.

Don't be overly strict or hard on yourself

Appreciate your strengths and embrace your weaknesses.

Have something to look forward to.

Last words:

Your life is a work in progress.

There are times when we have to recognise the possibility we may need help from sources other than just our family and friends. If you do feel interminably unhappy, you must help yourself get better and seek help from professional organisations or self-help groups.

You're never alone. Don't be alone.

Start every day saying 3 positive things.

Find where you want to go.

Offload the superfluous.

Carry only what you need.

Understand yourself.

Stop worrying.

FOCUS on your intent and the skip in your step will return naturally.

Disclaimer

This guide is designed to help give people a lift in life. To encourage them to see the positive in themselves and everything around them.

This work does not in any way presume to understand the deep and intricate psyche of the human mind. It is not designed to guarantee a cure for deep-rooted ailments or disorders. Individuals who have suffered bereavement or other serious forms of shock, loss or misfortune should not consider this guide as an authoritative cure for their symptoms of loss and would be advised to seek professional assistance.

This guide is intended solely as a form of self-help to individuals requiring encouragement and help in forming a more positive attitude to life.

Naturally the author is happy to help any such individuals find the correct help they may need.

Depression is a serous disorder and requires the correct treatment.

www.ingramcontent.com/pod-product-compliance
Lightning Source LLC
Chambersburg PA
CBHW060702030426
42337CB00017B/2718